Alien

Wastelanders

Matt Dickinson ◾ **Dynamo**

OXFORD
UNIVERSITY PRESS

TEAM X

Max, Cat, Ant and Tiger are four ordinary children with four extraordinary watches. When activated, their watches allow them to shrink to micro-size.

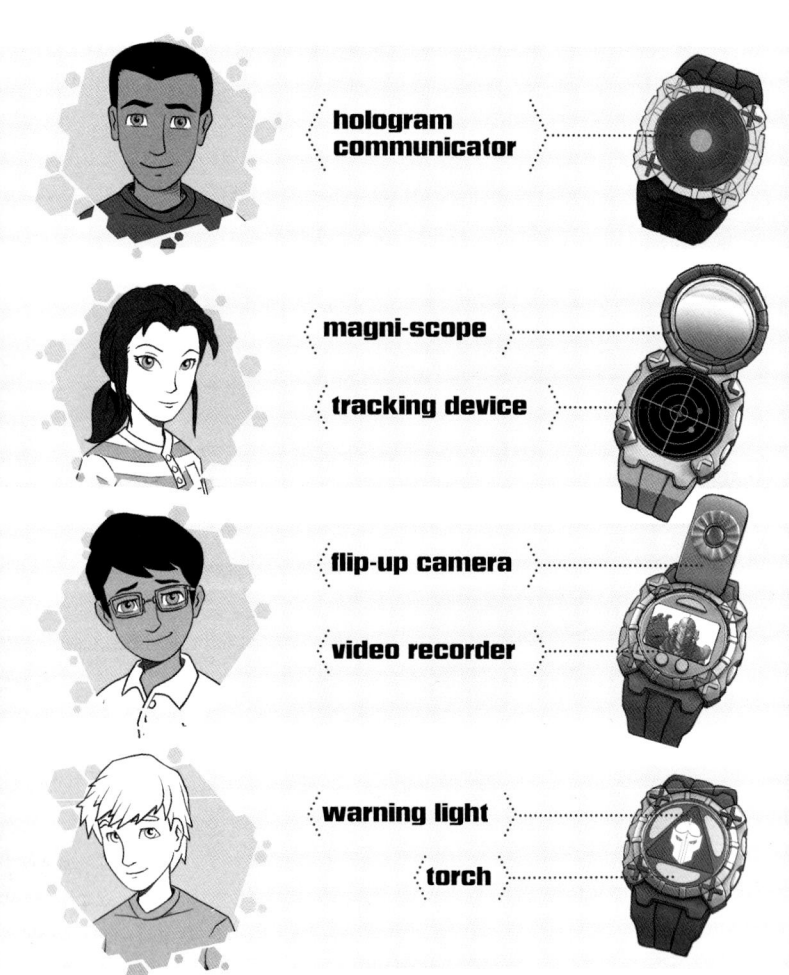

MAX — hologram communicator

CAT — magni-scope, tracking device

ANT — flip-up camera, video recorder

TIGER — warning light, torch

Previously ...

The watches were running low on power. Ant tried to recharge them using a machine that he had invented. However, during this process, something in the watches changed irrevocably.

When all the watches are synchronized, the micro-friends can travel through a rip in the fabric of space and time to other dimensions. Max, Cat, Ant and Tiger have become *rip-jumpers*.

Unfortunately, there is a problem. The rip has become permanently stuck open ... in Tiger's wardrobe! This leaves Earth – our Earth – open to attack.

A woman called **Perlest** came through the rip saying she wanted to help. She told the children that they needed to find the **Weaver**. Only he could seal the rip shut forever.

After many rip-jumps, the micro-friends found the Weaver, otherwise known as **Aracnan**. They took him back to their dimension. But it had all been a trick! The woman they knew as Perlest turned out to be her evil twin sister **Vilana**. She stole the Weaver's **Staff of Worlds**.

Now the children are trying to hunt down Vilana before she can use the Staff of Worlds to free her master, **Mordriss**, *The Dimension Reaper*.

Chapter 1 – Waste, waste everywhere

All four watches were synchronized. The portal was open. Max, Cat, Ant and Tiger were ready to rip-jump once more. As they stepped into the blue glow, the friends immediately perceived the strange distortion of space and time as it warped around them. Seconds later came the familiar shuffling of dimensions, like playing cards in a pack.

Then, just as quickly, the sensation changed again, and they felt themselves being sucked down as they plunged towards a new destination. The instant gravity reclaimed them, they began to fall, down and down towards a soft, but extremely smelly, landing.

Yuck! Cat thought, her senses overwhelmed. A gut-wrenching stink of rotting waste filled her nostrils. Then panic started to rise in her chest as she felt herself sinking under the surface of a slimy pit. Everything went dark. She thrashed her arms about, trying to swim upwards. For a few seconds she felt completely out of control as the air was squeezed out of her lungs. Someone's hand hit her head. Her elbow banged against a foot. Then her feet found something firm to push against and she managed to get some upwards movement.

Cat kicked and clawed her way up. As her head broke through the surface she took an enormous breath of air. She coughed and spluttered for a few moments, feeling a great surge of relief as Max and Tiger surfaced close by.

'Where's Ant?' Max asked with a gasp.

Cat and Tiger looked around in alarm. There was no sign of their friend. All they could see in any direction was a sea of rubbish. They had landed in a vast swamp-like dump.

Then they heard a cry for help, along with the sound of splashing. They waded towards the sound, eventually finding some solid ground and hauling themselves out of the swamp. The three friends scrambled over the rubbish until they found Ant, thrashing around in a pit filled with evil-smelling oil. He was stuck in it up to his waist, his lower body coated with congealed grease.

'Give me a hand,' Max yelled to the others.

Cat and Tiger joined him, reaching out to extricate Ant from the pit. It was difficult to get a firm grip on his oil-soaked clothes, but Max finally managed to grab him under the arms and, with the help of the other two, dragged him to more solid terrain.

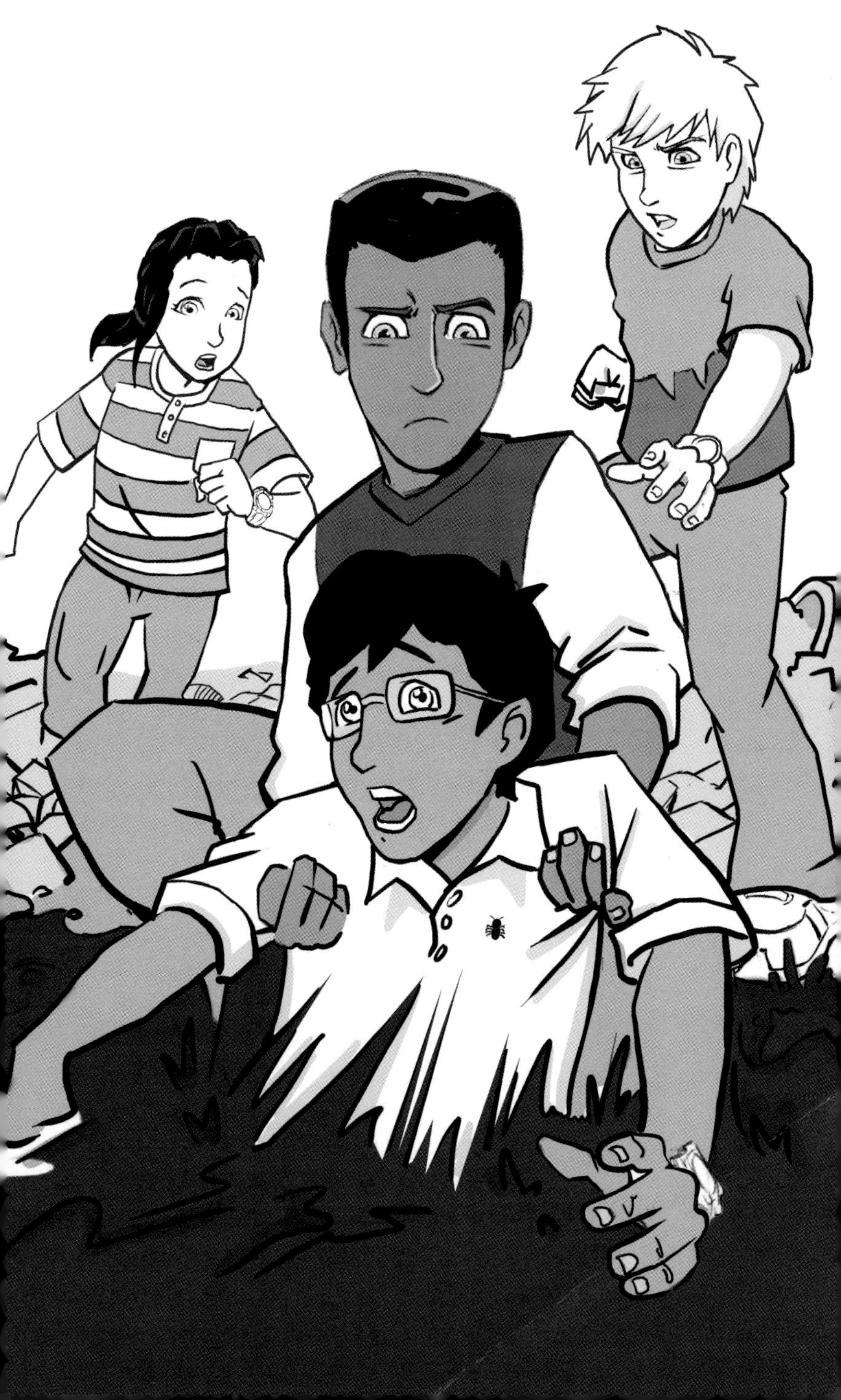

The four friends crouched on the ground, breathing hard, as they recovered from the rip-jump. They tried to clean themselves up a bit, brushing the rotting waste from their clothes.

'I feel dizzy,' Ant complained. He closed his eyes. 'And I can see flashing lights.'

Max and Cat exchanged a worried look. Cat put her hand on Ant's shoulder. 'Take a few deep breaths. You'll be OK. That was a really tough jump.'

None of them liked to mention it, but there was no doubt the rip-jumps were taking a heavy toll on their bodies. They felt their muscles aching with fatigue, a strange sense of dislocation, and an unpleasant pressure in their heads. Things were changing and not in a good way. And the four friends were getting further and further from home.

'We've rip-jumped into some kind of scrapyard,' Tiger said. 'Talk about bad luck.'

The view in every direction was menacing. The air was filled with a haze of acrid smoke. The place seemed completely unloved, as if nature had been squeezed out. There was no bird song to be heard; the only sign of life was the fat blowflies that buzzed around the rubbish piles.

'Check your watch, Cat,' Max suggested. 'See if you can pick up any trace of Vilana and the Staff of Worlds.'

Cat flipped up the screen of her watch and tuned the sensor until a faint luminous glow flickered on her tracker screen. 'She's here,' Cat announced. 'Well, somewhere in this dimension at least. But the signal is really faint.'

The four friends clambered up a bank of rubbish and fanned out to explore the immediate surroundings. Where there were gaps between the waste piles, they could see the terrain was stony and sterile; a rocky desert without a single green plant in view.

'I've found some tracks!' Tiger called out.

The others came to investigate, an uneasy silence falling between them as they tried to make sense of what they were seeing. Dotted around the junk stacks were a number of tyre tracks.

'Let's explore a bit more,' Max said. 'The sooner we can track down Vilana, the sooner we can get out of this place.'

The friends spread out again and began to weave through the junk. It was eerily quiet and their nerves were on high alert. The landscape seemed to offer no shortage of hiding places for hostile creatures, and the possibility of an ambush was impossible to ignore.

'Stay within shouting range of each other,' Max called. 'We mustn't get separated, whatever happens.'

Gradually the piles of junk got bigger and bigger, until the friends were moving between mounds that were almost the size of small hills.

'Let's try to get some height,' Ant suggested. The others agreed, and soon they were clambering up the side of one of the junk mountains, moving swiftly past the rusty, old engines, abandoned appliances and broken factory machinery that formed the pile. Within ten minutes they had reached the top of the scrapheap, where they found a most disheartening view.

'It's the same,' Cat said glumly. 'The same in every direction.'

She was right. The view was unrestricted across the rolling, rocky wasteland; wherever they turned, their eyes met the same depressing scene. Millions of tons of waste: spread everywhere.

'This dimension stinks,' Tiger observed.

Cat checked her watch once again, attempting to get a firm reading for Vilana. Although the luminous signal on her watch was stronger than before, it was still too weak to pinpoint Vilana's location.

'So, now what?' Max asked. 'Anyone got any ideas?'

'Look! There's smoke on the horizon.' Ant pointed towards a faint trickle of black fumes rising a long way off. 'There must be someone … or something … there to create it. We need to find out who lives here, and then we might pick up some clues about where Vilana is.'

Max thought back to the tracks they had found in the sand and a tremor of fear shivered up his back as his imagination raced, but he was determined not to show it. 'OK,' he agreed. 'We're not going to track Vilana down by standing on the top of this junk heap. So let's move.'

Chapter 2 – **The wastelanders**

The four friends descended the hill of rubbish and began the trek towards the smoke. Progress was slow as they picked their way between the piles of junk; the humid heat didn't help either.

'No sign of any fresh water,' Tiger lamented.

The sun was vicious when it managed to punch through the thick clouds. Brushing against a piece of metal rubbish was like touching the hob of a stove. Sweat was running in droplets down the back of their necks.

They crossed a small stream; it too was clogged up with toxic-smelling substances. The further they went, the more they saw that the sheer range of junk was astonishing. There were smashed-up cars and buses alongside ancient computers, redundant entertainment systems and black, plastic bags that smelled of rotten organic waste. Broken glass was everywhere, along with jagged shards of metal and millions of scattered nuts and bolts.

'I wonder how long it's been like this,' Cat said, looking around.

Ant shrugged. 'Hundreds of years maybe,' he guessed.

'It would probably take another hundred years to clean it up,' said Tiger. 'And an army of volunteers.'

Max wondered if a clean-up operation would even be possible: where would the junk go?

The four friends persisted with their journey, heading for the rising column of smoke which seemed to be the only sign of life. A couple of hours passed, and they hardly seemed to be any closer; picking a route through the endless rubbish was exhausting, and their strength was already low after the rip-jump. Then they crested a small rise and saw an extraordinary vision.

Below them, hidden in a small valley of rubbish, was a jewel of a lake, with crystal-clear waters and vivid green rushes growing on the sandy shores. A small flock of white egrets was feeding in the shallows.

Tiger rubbed his eyes. 'Am I dreaming this?' he asked. 'Or is that fresh water down there?'

'It certainly looks like it!' Ant confirmed. 'But how has it survived all the pollution?'

'Who cares?' laughed Tiger. 'Let's go and drink.'

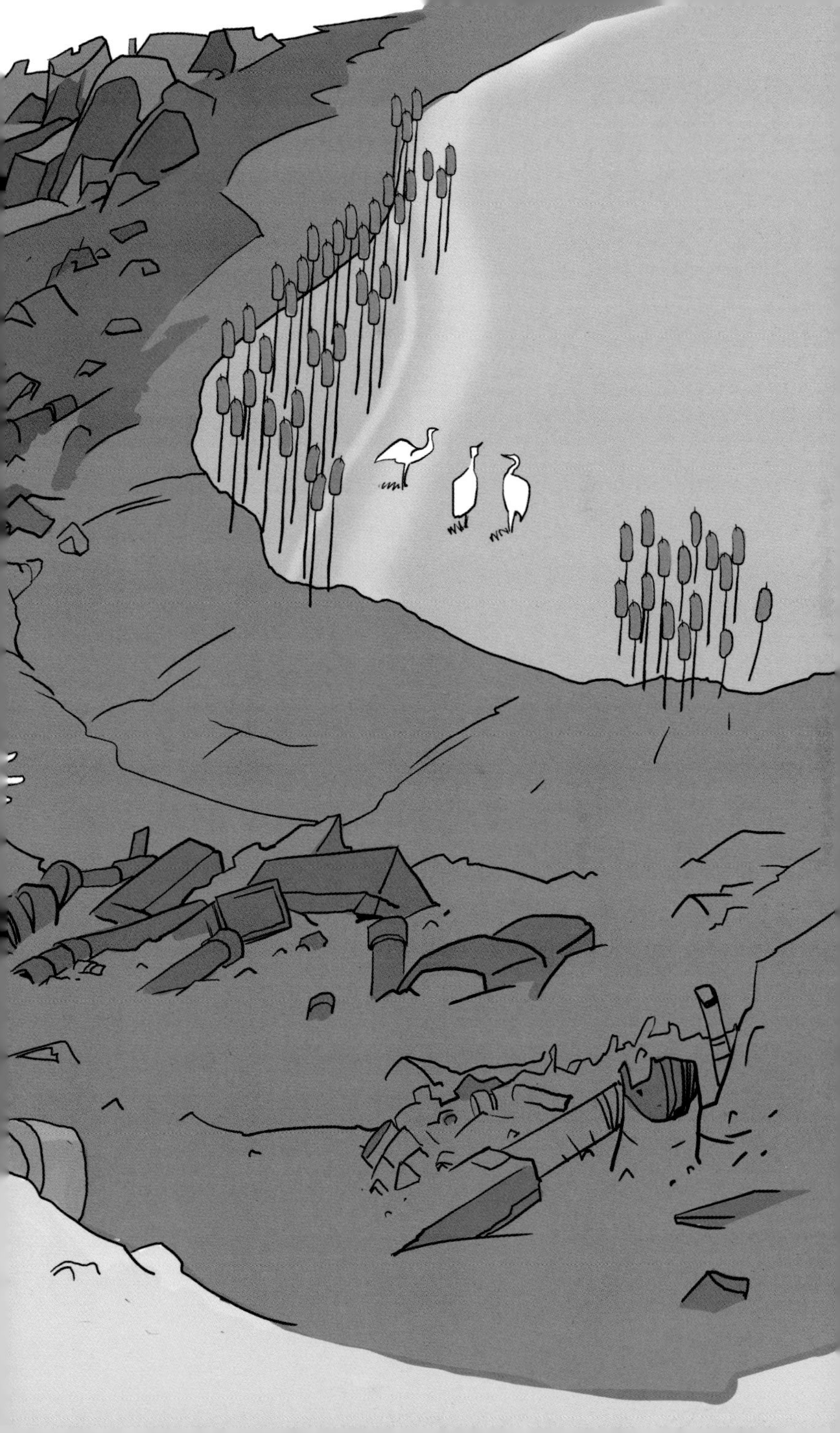

The four friends were about to rush down to the lake to slake their thirst when Tiger's watch suddenly flashed a red warning light.

'I've got a danger alert,' he said.

They all skidded to a halt and looked around warily. A distant rumbling sound began to reach them.

'I can't see anything,' Ant said. 'But I can definitely *smell* something.'

Cat wrinkled her nose as a new and terrible smell of rotting substances suddenly wafted over them. 'What's *that*?'

'Blurgh!' Tiger exclaimed, pinching his nose. 'That is disgusting!'

'Rotting meat!' Max sniffed.

'Six-month-old fish!' Ant added.

'Dead rats!' Tiger concluded ominously.

The noise they had heard in the distance became more distinct: it was the rumbling of an engine somewhere above them. They scanned the skies looking for it, but the clouds of dense pollution made it impossible to catch a glimpse of the craft.

'There's some sort of transporter up there,' Max said, 'and I'm guessing from the smell that it's filled with waste.'

The sound of propulsion jets got closer. And, as

the smell gradually intensified, the sand around the crystal-clear lake seemed to ripple. Then hundreds of shapes began to vibrate around the shores of the lake as humanoid forms emerged.

'Are those people buried in the sand?' Cat gasped.

One by one, the figures shook themselves free of sand and rushed silently to the water-side.

'The noise of that transporter has brought them out,' Ant observed.

As they watched, the shores of the lake started to fill with the strange-looking figures. They were dressed in scraps of leather and denim that seemed to be filthy with oil. Quickly, they came together, working in unison to unearth two huge winches from the ground. There was the sound of a motor and great chains began to tug at a hidden structure. Little by little, a protective cover was pulled over the lake – a canopy camouflaged with painted rocks and rubbish which perfectly matched the ground. Soon the lake was completely hidden from aerial view.

'It's like a roof on a stadium,' Cat said with admiration. 'They've made the lake vanish in two minutes flat!'

'They're protecting it!' Max said in awe.

It was an incredible display of teamwork and, as the aerial transporter emerged through the clouds of pollution, the curious figures silently vanished back into the sand.

The four friends dived for cover behind a big pile of scrap as the vast transporter appeared, its dark outline forming a sinister silhouette in the polluted air. As it laboriously passed overhead, the smell got progressively worse. The huge craft kept going for a while; then, a short distance away, it began to hover. There was the sound of metallic doors grinding open, then countless tons of rotting, organic waste was expelled from chutes that stuck out of the bottom and back of the craft, splattering on the ground and creating a foul cloud of noxious vapour that immediately started to spread.

'That is the worst thing I have ever smelled in my life!' Cat said, as her eyes filled up with tears. 'Why do they treat this place so badly?'

'Because the roaches make money from dumping waste,' came a voice behind them. 'And the more junk that gets dumped here, the richer they become!'

The four friends whipped round in surprise, finding themselves face to face with a girl. She was dressed, like the people who had emerged from the sand, in handmade clothes of leather and denim, and wore a cap pulled down over her scruffy, brown hair. She looked about twelve years old, but it was a bit difficult to tell.

'My name is Seny,' she told them. 'Where have you come from? We don't get many holidaymakers round here.'

'It's … complicated,' Cat replied. 'But don't worry: we don't want to hurt you.'

Seny frowned at this, looking suspicious.

'We saw the way you protected the lake. That was an amazing bit of teamwork,' Max hurriedly continued.

'Us wastelanders look out for each other,' Seny said proudly. 'We learned a long time ago that it's the only way to survive.'

'Wastelanders?' Tiger repeated.

'That's our clan,' Seny continued. 'We're known as the wastelanders because we recycle waste as best we can and try to keep out of the way of the roaches.'

'Who are the roaches?' Ant asked.

'An ancient human society that has gradually manipulated its gene pool to take on cockroach-like characteristics.'

Cat frowned. 'Why would they do that?'

'Because nothing survives like a cockroach can. Some people say they're the only creatures tough enough to survive a nuclear war. And they can live off any type of waste,' Seny explained.

'How big are they?' Ant asked, fascinated.

'Big enough,' Seny said ominously. 'You'll come across them if you hang around long enough.'

'Well, we're not planning on being here for long,' Cat told her. 'Just long enough to find someone – a woman called Vilana. Have you heard of her?'

'No. But we can ask around in the settlement.' Seny gestured for them to follow, then led the way down to the shores of the lake.

Now the craft was gone, the artificial canopy had been rolled back so that the lake was revealed once again. As they got closer to the aquamarine waters, the friends were amazed to see life teeming here in the midst of a toxic wasteland. A special wall had been built around the lake to stop polluted water seeping in, and the water was so clear they could see to a depth of many metres. Huge, healthy-looking fish and other freshwater creatures swam lazily to and fro. It was a little oasis of calm in the midst of a hellish landscape.

'The Lake of the Ancestors,' Seny told them. 'The

last unpolluted place on the planet, and the only remaining source of fresh drinking water and good protein. That's why we guard it with our lives!'

'What about the roaches? Don't they need to drink?' Ant asked.

Seny laughed morosely. 'They've adapted themselves over generations to match the dimension perfectly. Drinking polluted water is sheer pleasure to them, and the more rotten the food, the more they like it.'

'So why do you have to hide the lake from them?' Max asked.

'Because they want to destroy us. And, little by little, they are winning. The community around this lake is the last wastelander stronghold; if the roaches knew the precise location of this lake, they would fill it with toxic chemicals in the blink of an eye.'

Seny beckoned to the friends and led them to a seemingly blank section of sand. 'Would you like to meet some of my people? See if they have heard of this … Vilana?'

'OK,' said Max. The others nodded their agreement.

'Follow me!' she said and, with a cheeky smile, she jumped forward and disappeared into the ground, seemingly swallowed up by the sand. It disconcerted the friends.

'How did she do that?' Tiger asked. 'Is it quicksand?'

'It's a cool trick,' Cat said in admiration.

Max looked suspicious. 'It might be a trap.'

'I don't think so.' Ant poked his foot into the sand where the girl had vanished into, watching in amazement as his foot was effortlessly swallowed up. 'It seems to be a type of doorway.'

'Here goes!' Tiger took a great leap and vanished through the sand in the same way as Seny had. Taking a deep breath, his friends followed him into the unknown.

Chapter 3 – Surveillance

The four friends crashed in a heap on to the floor of a substantial underground cavern. Seny laughed at them as they untangled their limbs and climbed to their feet. Then they stood, brushing stray grains of sand off their clothes, and looked around at the interior of the cave. It was a welcoming place compared to the chaos of the upper world, illuminated by a gentle, golden light. There were large, brightly coloured cushions scattered around to sit on.

'Welcome to my home,' Seny said. 'Here, a nice, cool drink will help.' She thrust a clay container into each waiting hand. The friends gulped down the sweetest, freshest water they had ever tasted.

'How come the sand doesn't just fall into the hole?' Ant asked, as he stared up at the sand door they had just fallen through.

'It's a sand membrane,' Seny told them proudly. 'Sand mixed with latex and thirty different types of polymer resins. Human bodies can slip through it, and it reforms immediately to get back its shape. You'd be amazed by what you can do with sand once you've had a few thousand years to experiment with it.'

The friends looked at each other, impressed. The wastelanders had mastered their environment in some very inventive ways.

'Let me show you more,' Seny suggested.

The tour of the wastelander underground village began, gradually revealing to the four friends the extraordinary scale of the settlement. Tunnels had been cut in all directions, some for living and sleeping in, others for teaching classes of wastelander children, and even some 'greenhouse' tunnels in which rows of healthy plants were growing under banks of ultraviolet lights. There weren't many adults around, but Seny explained they would have gone out 'scrap surfing' after the last transporter dump – that is, hunting through the latest junk for useful bits and pieces which could be recycled.

'If it were down to us, we would try to turn this place back to what it was before – a fertile and healthy land,' Seny told them. 'But we fear it is too late to turn back the clock. The roaches have done too much damage.'

'How many of them are there – roaches, I mean?' Max asked.

'Oh, there are colonies everywhere now. It's impossible to say.'

Seny pushed open a door a crack to show the friends the room where two wastelander adults – a man and a woman – were watching TV monitors.

'What are they doing?' asked Ant.

'Monitoring our early warning system,' Seny replied. 'The system is made from recycled TVs and repaired security cameras.' She pointed to the bank of screens. 'There's a camera pointing in every direction. As soon as the roaches get anywhere near the lake we spot them and close up the canopy.'

One of the adults flicked a switch and a new image emerged: a city scene filled with moving creatures. They were repulsive-looking beings, with bloated, almost human, torsos and legs, but with heads which were equipped with antennae and bulbous, compound eyes.

'That's them. The roaches,' Seny whispered. 'This camera is a secret one we planted in the heart of Roach City.'

'Those are the ugliest creatures we've seen so far!' Tiger exclaimed.

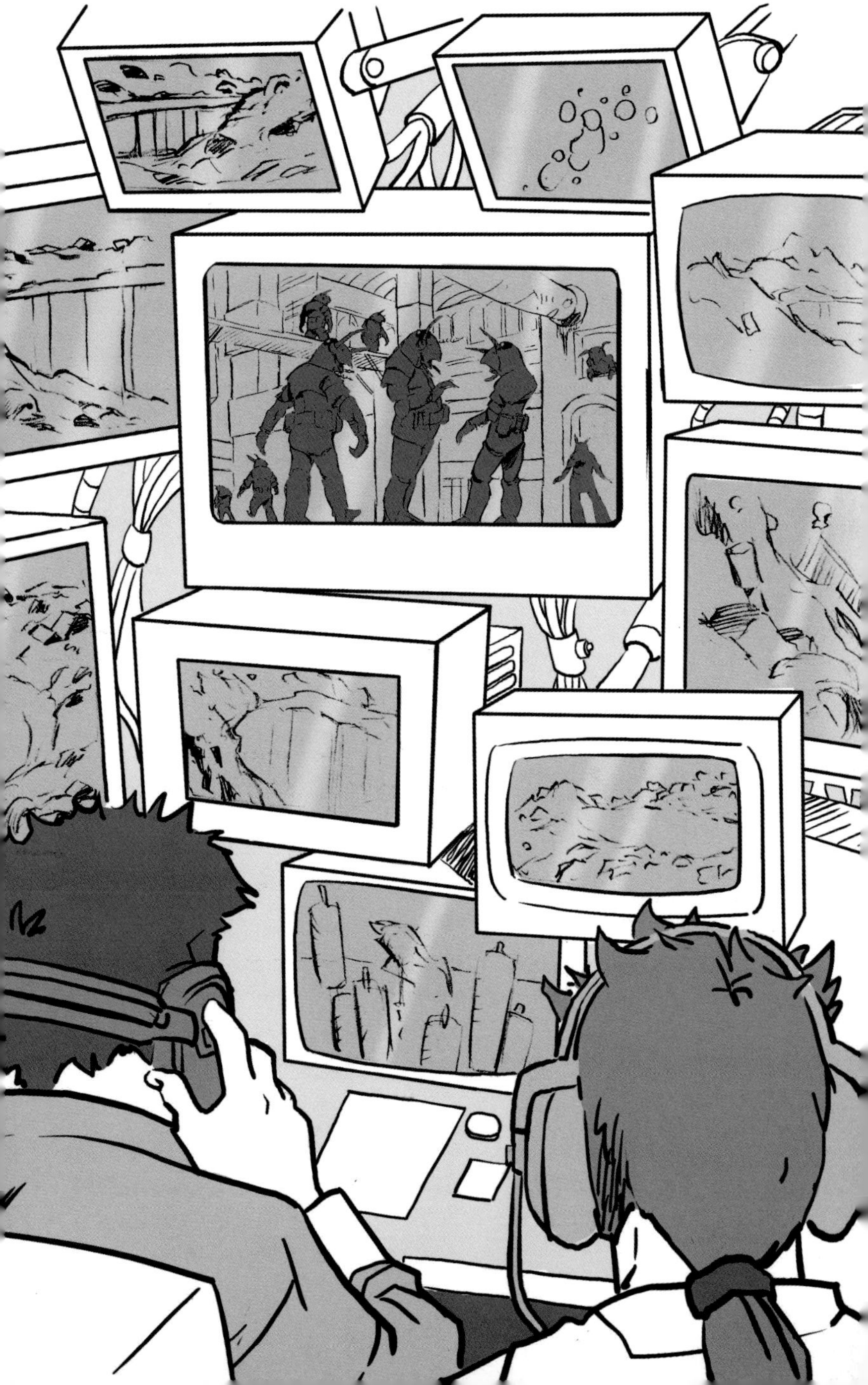

'I don't doubt it,' Seny laughed. 'But don't underestimate them. They can be ruthless when they want to be.'

Seny gestured for her new friends to follow her into the room. 'Have you seen any unusual visitors in the city lately?' she asked the surveillance team.

'We did see something,' the woman replied. 'A big procession yesterday morning. Here, look …' She rewound through a surveillance tape and found the footage she was looking for. It showed a convoy of vehicles passing through the centre of the city. In the back of one of the vehicles, the friends saw the profile of a familiar figure. Seny glanced over her shoulder and saw Cat nod.

'Freeze the image there,' Seny said to the woman.

The friends found themselves staring at a fuzzy image of their nemesis.

'Vilana,' Ant murmured. 'At least we know we're getting close.' It was a chilling moment for all four of them; they knew that locating Vilana was only part of their mission. The tough part would be *stopping* her and getting the Staff of Worlds back.

'Why are you searching for that woman?' Seny asked the friends, as she led them back to her dwelling. 'She looks terrifying.'

There was an awkward pause as Max hesitated. Then he decided to open up; Seny had shared so much with them, after all. So he told her their story as briefly as he could.

'You've got a dangerous mission ahead,' Seny said, after Max had finished. 'The only way to find Vilana is to go right into Roach City.'

'Can you help us to get there?' Cat asked.

Seny thought for a moment, then beckoned for the four of them to follow once more. She took them back up on to the surface and away from the lake. A short walk between the rubbish heaps brought them to what looked like the burial place of dozens of wrecked vehicles including racing cars and dune buggies.

'You'll need some wheels,' she told them. 'And the faster the better.'

'Now you're talking!' said Tiger, looking around him. 'But from this lot?' He gestured to a stack of utterly destroyed machines.

The four friends wandered among the wrecks, grim-faced.

'I've been working on one with my father,' Seny told them. 'You can take it if you can help me finish it off.' She led them over to a part-finished, four-seater dune buggy with its wheels half-buried in sand. Then she uncovered a toolkit that she'd hidden below the surface not far away.

'Needs a bit of tender loving care,' Cat observed with a wry smile.

Max walked round the back of the buggy. 'It still has an engine,' he said, as he ran his hands over the weathered metal. 'And the chassis looks OK.'

'I'll take first drive,' Tiger said, jumping in the driving seat and clutching the steering wheel. The others smiled as they saw the unmistakable glint of adrenaline in his eyes.

'We'll have to get it going first,' Cat reminded him.

Ant banged on the fuel tank, getting a metallic echo in return. 'What about fuel?' He unscrewed the cap and peered inside. 'This tank is well and truly empty.'

'I'll go and get some,' Seny offered. 'We scavenge it drop by drop from the vehicles as soon as they get dumped.'

Seny headed back to the settlement to pick up the fuel while the friends got to work. Max and Ant checked the engine while Cat and Tiger excavated the wheels from the encroaching sand.

'Looks like it's been through a battle or two,' Ant said, brushing some sand off one of the dented front panels.

'It's a survivor!' Tiger exclaimed. 'Like us. And that's what we need right now.'

They started to move some of the rubbish that had collected inside the car and made an unwelcome discovery. The broken-off wooden shaft of a spear was embedded in the passenger seat.

'Ouch,' Cat said. 'I think we might have discovered what happened to the previous owners.'

Max pulled the spear free, revealing a vicious-looking spearhead with a razor-sharp serrated edge. 'This has to belong to the roaches,' he said. 'At least now we know what type of weapons they use.'

Soon Seny returned, lugging a fuel can. Once the fuel tank was replenished, Tiger climbed into the driver's seat. One turn of the ignition key deflated their enthusiasm: nothing happened.

'It must be the battery,' Tiger said. 'Sounds totally flat.'

A further ten minutes' scavenging found a battery of the same size in another abandoned vehicle.

'Let's hope this one has a bit of charge,' said Max. He connected the battery and Tiger tried again.

'Yes!' The engine turned with a reluctant groan – but quickly spluttered and died again.

Just then a siren blasted out.

'A roach raiding party is on the way!' Seny told them urgently. She looked to the horizon where a cloud of dust signalled a convoy of roach vehicles on the move.

The lakeside quickly erupted into activity.

'Must be looking for something important … They don't normally come in such large numbers,' she continued.

Cat had a horrible feeling that she knew what the something important might be.

Them.

Chapter 4 – Roach attack!

The four friends looked in the direction Seny was pointing. Dozens of brilliantly lit buggy headlights were zooming towards them across the wasteland.

'You have to get moving. And keep moving!' she told them. 'Roach City is ten miles due east across the dunes. If you get there you might be able to lose them. Good luck!' And with that, she turned and ran back to the settlement just as the canopy was sliding into place over the lake.

Seconds later, she joined the rest of the wastelanders in their underground world, vanishing beneath the sands in a flash. The transformation was brilliant: no one would ever know the wastelanders were concealed there.

'Come on!' Max said. 'We need to get some life in this thing.'

Tiger turned the ignition key. The engine turned over again, but nothing happened.

'Maybe we can jump-start it?' Ant suggested.

Max and Cat joined him at the back of the buggy.

'Push!' shouted Max.

They shoved the vehicle as hard as they could towards a nearby rocky slope. Not far away they could hear the, fast-approaching, roach buggies, the engines revving madly as the insectoid creatures weaved in and out of the rubbish piles.

'We've got about a minute!' Cat told the others.

They pushed their buggy over the edge of the slope, and it started to gain its own momentum. As it picked up speed, Max jumped in the front and Cat and Ant leapt into the back. For several anxious moments it seemed the engine would never fire up. Great clouds of black smoke spewed out of the exhaust.

'We've been spotted!' Cat shouted, glancing over her shoulder. The raiders had turned directly towards the friends, the rumble of their powerful engines sending sinister vibrations through the ground.

'Come on!' shouted Tiger in frustration as they neared the bottom of the slope.

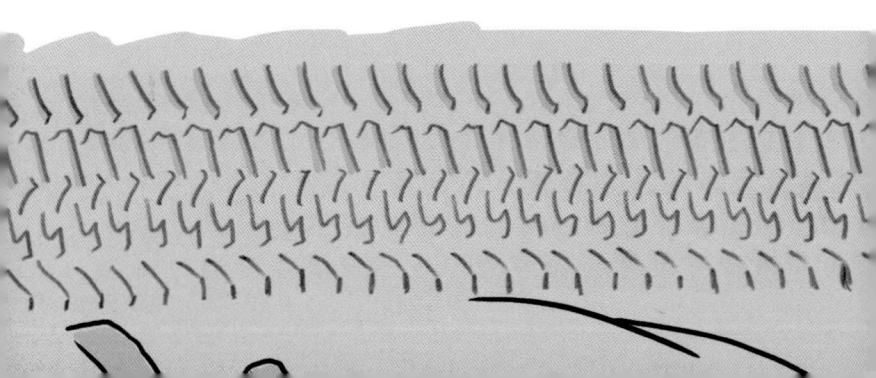

An instant later the buggy kicked into life with a gratifying roar. The engine was so loud Ant had to cover his ears against the noise. Tiger put his foot on the accelerator, and the vehicle lurched forward with a breathtaking surge of power. They clung on to the roll cage for dear life for a few seconds.

'Better fasten up those harnesses,' Tiger told them. 'This is going to be a bumpy ride.'

Max, Cat and Ant snapped their shoulder harnesses securely into place.

Tiger stamped on the clutch and pushed the gearstick aggressively forward. A loud crunching noise came from the gearbox, and the buggy kangarooed forward a few metres before coming to a halt as the engine stalled.

'Whoops!' Tiger fired the engine up again, repeated the manoeuvre, more delicately this time, and selected gear successfully. He gave the others a nervous smile.

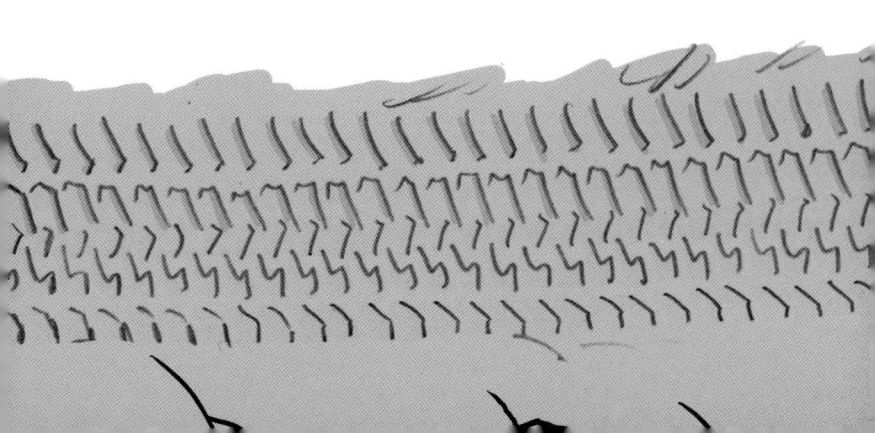

The buggy quickly picked up speed again, but the horde of roach buggies was closing in horribly fast. The friends could hear the strangely high-pitched whistles and cries of the excited creatures, even over the throaty roar of their engines.

Within a couple of minutes, the raiders were almost upon them. The furious creatures were leaning out of their vehicles, waving their spears as they approached.

'You weren't kidding about these creatures being the ugliest we've ever seen!' Ant shouted to Tiger.

Suddenly the friends felt a violent impact to the back of the buggy. One of the roach raiders had rammed into them at high speed. The blow sent them weaving across the precipitous edge of a dune, sending the buggy up on its two outer wheels.

'Ahhhhhh!' All four friends let out a cry of fear.

Then Tiger turned into the skid, managing to regain control as the two airborne tyres crashed back to the sand. The friends flashed a shocked glance at each other: the impact had been severe, and it was easy to imagine how another blow could cause them to tumble completely out of control.

'I've heard of a white-knuckle ride,' Cat said, 'but this is ridiculous!'

Two more roach raiders came in on either side. A spear zipped overhead, missing Ant by a fraction and stabbing into the sand at the side of the buggy. Tiger found a bit more speed from somewhere and the buggy pulled fractionally ahead.

A straight-line trajectory was impossible: piles of scrap were everywhere, making the driving challenge even more extreme. Old turbines, stacks of giant rubber tyres, panels of charred plastic: it was a constant obstacle course. The buggy turned first one way then another as Tiger kept them ahead, his foot pushed down hard on the accelerator, blinking the sand from his eyes as he kept the momentum going.

'The dunes are getting steeper!' Cat warned. Suddenly they were airborne – driving right off the razor-edged ridge of a monster dune and catching air for a few moments before crashing down to earth again. The suspension springs of the buggy creaked with the strain as they bounced once … twice … then regained control.

'Coming in from the right!' Ant yelled.

A roach buggy manoeuvred alongside them, the roach co-pilot grabbing an oil thrower and aiming right at the buggy.

Tiger swerved as a heavy plume of jet-black oil arced through the air and spattered on to the back of their vehicle.

'Faster, Tiger!' Ant urged him. 'If they hit us with that stuff you won't be able to see a thing.'

'I'm giving it everything,' Tiger replied. The buggy's engine was already steaming under the strain and smoke was starting to ascend from the glowing body. The friends could smell the oil heating up as it sizzled on the metal chassis.

In the near distance a new vision suddenly appeared: a huge lake filled with glutinous, black oil. From it came occasional flares of dull-red flames as bubbles broke the surface and spontaneously combusted. Behind it the four friends could see the remains of a city, a broken relic of a place.

'That must be the outskirts of Roach City,' Cat yelled.

Tiger began to steer for the ruins; the roach raiders were still neck and neck with them.

As they reached the banks of the black lake, one of the roach vehicles mounted another attack with an oil gun.

This time Tiger yanked the steering wheel to the left, sideswiping the roach buggy and sending it plunging into the lake with a greasy splash. As they had no harnesses, the impact sent the roach raiders cannoning out of their seats, legs wiggling with panic as they flew through the air, only to plummet right into the middle of the glutinous sludge.

'Yes!' Cat cried, as she saw the hapless roaches struggling miserably for the shore.

Soon the friends were hurtling along the concrete remains of old streets that made up the outskirts of the city. It was a bizarre, apocalyptic vision.

'We're not going to shake them all – where can we hide?' Max said. There were still half a dozen roach raiders not far behind them.

'Look! Over there!' Ant pointed to a dark archway set into the ground. Next to it was a battered and weathered sign which read simply: *Underground*. 'There might be old tunnels we can hide in!'

'Go for it!' Max told Tiger.

'Whatever you say!' Tiger swerved across the abandoned roadway and drove straight into the tunnel. The change of direction caught some of the roach drivers by surprise – they collided in a twisted heap of metal as they tried to follow.

Ant cheered. 'That's three less to worry about!'

Tiger clicked on the buggy's powerful spotlights as they crashed down a stairway at high speed.

'There's … still … a … few … on … our … tail,' Cat yelled, the bumps from the stairs distorting her voice.

Ant glanced behind as they zoomed through a derelict ticket concourse. One of the roaches in the lead buggy was getting ready to shoot another great plume of noxious oil.

'Faster!' Ant yelled.

'I'm trying my best!' Tiger bellowed in reply.

The buggy tilted to the right as Tiger drove on to an old platform. They were briefly airborne; then the vehicle crunched down on to the disused tracks. Tiger accelerated into the tunnel, the buggy juddering along railway sleepers.

Soon they passed a huge metal door: an ancient defence system to stop the tunnels getting submerged in a flood. It was exactly the size and shape to fill the circular profile of the tunnel.

'The stations can be sealed off with these doors,' Ant called out. 'All we have to do is get them closed and the roaches won't be able to follow us.'

'That's *all* we have to do?' cried Cat. 'Those doors look seriously heavy and they might not have been moved for hundreds of years.'

'I think it's a good idea,' Max said. 'Next time we come to a door we'll give it a try – we haven't exactly got anything to lose.'

Chapter 5 – **Snatched**

Two more abandoned stations flashed past. The roach chase team showed no signs of capitulating, but Tiger managed to accelerate to widen the gap between them. Then he skidded to a halt at the next of the metal doors.

'Quickly!' Max yelled, unclipping his harness and jumping out.

Cat, Ant and Tiger jumped out after him and ran to the heavy steel door, trying not to think about the roach raiders who were getting closer by the second. It took all their power to start the metal door moving on its hinges, but finally it began swinging, emitting a great rusty groan as it did so.

'Push harder!' Cat urged the others.

The gap in the doorway was narrowing fast, but so was the distance between the friends and the roach raiders. Now the lead vehicles were skidding to a stop. The door was nearly closed when the first roach slipped through the gap.

'Watch out, Max!'

It all happened incredibly quickly. The roach acted with lightning speed, grabbing Max by the arm. Within a second, Max had been yanked through the gap and was being bundled into the back of one of the roach buggies.

'Close the door!' Max screamed. Even at the moment of maximum peril he was thinking of the safety of his friends.

Another roach approached the gap and tried to squeeze through to grab Ant, but Cat and Tiger managed to slam the door closed before he could get through. The tunnel was sealed. Moments later, they heard the ominous sound of the buggy engines moving away.

'That's it,' Tiger said miserably. 'Max is gone. They've got him as a hostage. How are we going to get him back?'

Cat squinted into the darkness ahead of them. 'We'll just have to find another way out. There's no time to lose – we have to find him as fast as we can.'

An hour later Tiger found a safe exit out of the underground system and they were back in the polluted, uninviting world of the blighted dimension.

There was no sign of the roach raiding party.

And no sign of Max.

* * * * * *

Max, meanwhile, was being transported into the heart of Roach City. He was tied up in the back of one of the roach buggies, bruised and utterly terrified from the high-speed journey. The jubilant roaches were beeping their horns and klaxons as they sped towards the centre of their capital, clearly delighted to have captured their prize.

Then Max heard a walkie-talkie crackle and a horribly familiar voice cut through the air. 'Did you capture one?' It was Vilana, the harsh tone of her voice easily audible above the engine noise.

'Yes! We have a prisoner,' came the reply from one roach.

Vilana was waiting for Max. But what did she want from him? *They* were supposed to be after *her*. Then the realization hit him. There was only one thing she could want from him: his watch. That was why the roaches had been happy with just one hostage. They were acting under Vilana's instructions; one prisoner was enough. It made perfect sense. Vilana knew all too well that the power to create the rip came only when their four watches were all *together*. By stealing Max's watch from him and destroying it, she would consign him and his friends to an eternity in this junkyard dimension. Their fate would be entirely in her hands.

It was a truly awful prospect, not least because it would leave Vilana free to continue her mission with the Staff of Worlds: a mission that would only end when she freed her master Mordriss from his prison at Dimensions' End.

'Just five minutes and you will be with our mistress!' the roach shouted gleefully to Max.

Max looked up. They were approaching a fortified monstrosity made entirely from scrap. Every single dwelling was constructed from used rubber tyres and sheets of corrugated iron held together with a black, tar-like substance.

The clock was ticking. He had to act now. Max closed his eyes, trying to make it look like he had fainted, whilst secretly twisting his wrist so that he could get access to his watch. He pushed his body against the looped cords that bound him but found he could not get his right hand into a good position to release the watch strap. He kept trying, but it was awkward with the bucking and bouncing motion of the buggy.

Max summoned all his strength and pushed as hard as he could against the cords. He won a bit more movement and managed to get his fingers underneath his watch strap. The buckle was tight against the skin of his wrist but, at long last, he did manage to slip it free so that the watch was dangling in his fingers.

Now. What to do with it? Max realized he had very few options: he could try and secrete the watch in a hiding place on the buggy in the hope he could retrieve it later, or he could drop the watch and make a mental note of the location to find it if he managed to escape. If he didn't manage to escape, Cat could track its location with her watch – then at least his friends could make it out of this dismal dimension without him.

Both options were risky. And time was against him, because, in that moment, the buggies raced through the gates and entered a great dusty square. Max was forced to close his fingers over the watch as the roaches began to race round and round in a crazy circle, their unearthly cries causing more and more of their kind to emerge from their dwellings.

Max felt himself elevated in the air as the roaches dragged him from the vehicle. Then he was dumped in the dirt in the middle of the square. He clutched at the watch, realizing he had to act now or not at all. Using his body as cover, he surreptitiously scooped a few handfuls of sand away from the ground. Then, disguising his movements as best he could, he dropped the watch into the hole and smoothed the sand back over it so it was completely buried. Fortunately, none of the roaches spotted the action.

Soon a mini tornado began to whirl in the centre of the square. Gradually the whirlwind of dust and rubbish picked up speed and became more powerful. A spine-tingling high-pitched wailing came from the wind as the circulating mass of air filled the whole square. Then, just as suddenly as it had begun, it dwindled, and an elegant dark-haired woman emerged from the dust cloud. The roach crowd went quiet. Her appearance was chilling in the extreme: her pale complexion and piercing blue eyes set off perfectly by her white suit. In her hand was the Staff of Worlds.

'Vilana,' Max muttered.

'So nice to see you again,' she said, with a cackle of laughter. Then turning to one of the roach guards, she commanded, 'Untie the worm!'

Worm? Max thought. In this dimension being a worm wouldn't be such a bad option, at least compared to being a roach. *Keep thinking stupid thoughts like that*, Max urged himself. He knew that keeping his sense of humour intact would be a good weapon against interrogation.

Max was roughly manhandled as his bonds were released. Then he was dragged to his feet. He stood there for a few moments as the blood ran back into his legs, trying not to show the pain this caused. Claws pushed at the small of his back, and a sarcastic cheer rippled around the square as he was jostled forward a few paces. Finally he stood right in front of Vilana, staring up at her defiantly and doing his best to conceal his fear.

'You see what happens when you set yourself up as the *leader*?' Vilana spat. 'You make yourself the perfect target.'

'I don't set myself up to be anything,' Max replied bravely. 'I just try to help my friends.'

'Well they'll be *lost* without you now, won't they?' Vilana laughed. 'And when I have your watch, your rip-jumping days will be over, and I will be free to continue my own mission without the worry of *distractions*.'

'We will find a way to follow you,' Max asserted. 'You can be sure of that.'

His words had real bravado, but inside he had no idea how they could ever follow and defeat Vilana without all four of their precious devices.

Then Vilana noticed his bare wrist. A flash of rage crossed her face. 'Where is your watch?' she snapped. 'I haven't got time to hang about in this stinking dimension.'

Max took a step backwards. 'Somewhere you'll never find it.' He carefully avoided looking at the place he had buried the watch.

For a moment, Vilana's face creased up, then instead of shouting, she laughed. 'Never mind if the watch is lost,' she said. 'In any case, you are powerless without it. And there's somewhere special I want to take you …'

Vilana swiftly used her staff to open up a rip. Max struggled as hard as he could, but there were too many guards holding him. Vilana thrust him towards the portal, then stepped in after him as he was swallowed up into an unknown void.

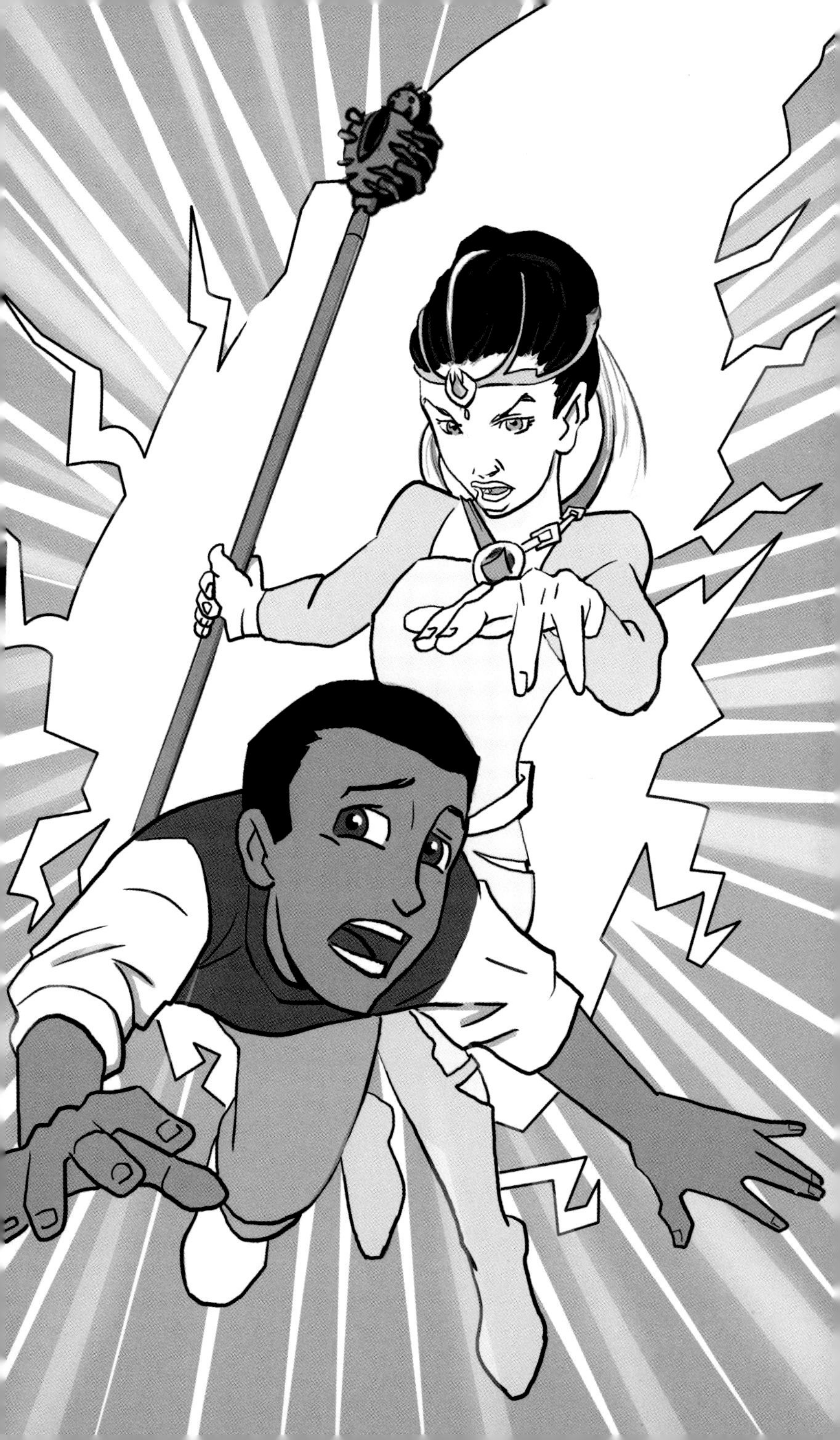

Chapter 6 – The tower of broken mirrors

In the city's derelict outskirts, Cat, Ant and Tiger were driving as fast as they could towards the heart of Roach City. Cat was tracking the signal from Max's watch. The signal was weak, but at least it gave them a compass bearing to follow.

Then Cat felt her watch vibrate. 'I've just detected a new rip,' she called over the noise of the engine. 'A portal has just opened up.'

Tiger glanced over at Cat's watch to see the telltale signal on her screen. 'Could Vilana have left the dimension?'

'Possibly.'

'Well, we still need to go to Roach City even if Vilana has left,' Tiger reasoned. 'If we find Max's watch, we find Max, right?'

'Right!' The thought of finding Max was enough to fill the friends with a renewed determination, even though the risks of going into the roach settlement would be extreme.

Tiger accelerated again and they homed in on

Roach City, racing as fast as they dared, horribly aware that every second was vital in the quest to free Max.

When they neared the inner city wall, Tiger found a place where the buggy could be hidden: a hollow in the ground which was deep enough to drive into. The three friends scavenged sheets of corrugated iron that had been dumped on the sand nearby, piling them on top of the buggy to disguise it from passing roach patrols.

'Shrink?' Ant asked.

Cat and Tiger nodded. They knew it was their only realistic chance of getting into the city unnoticed.

The three friends set their watches and shrank, then sprinted away from the disguised buggy and crawled through the barricade of junk that acted as the inner city wall. They kept to the murky shadows of the waste piles, zig-zagging through a maze of rubbish-filled streets as they pursued the signal on Cat's watch.

Danger was everywhere: roach buggies were racing recklessly down the narrow alleys, roach juveniles were playing happily on the waste piles. Twice the micro-friends were forced to dive for cover into putrid piles of unknown organic material.

'If anyone knows what this stuff is,' Ant said after they emerged from one particularly disgusting mess of sludge, 'please don't tell me!'

Soon they reached a spot where the signal was maximum strength: a broad dusty square with plenty of roaches walking about.

'It's strange,' Cat observed. 'The signal says Max's watch is right there in the middle of the square.'

The three of them scanned every corner of the square from their position, crouched beside an upturned bin, but there was no sign of Max at all.

'We need to get closer,' said Cat.

The problem was that the location was exposed and open. If they attempted to retrieve the watch, they would be spotted immediately by the roaches, even at micro-size.

'I've got an idea,' Tiger volunteered. 'There's plenty of old boxes and stuff blowing around. Why don't we get ourselves under a box and slowly head out there? They won't notice us amongst the huge amount of rubbish strewn across the square.'

The others agreed to the tactic, and they quickly found an abandoned cardboard box to use as cover. Luckily there were already some small rips in the box that they could use for observation. Holding the box above their heads, they manoeuvred cautiously across to the area where the signal was strongest.

When the signal stopped flashing, Cat said, 'We're right on top of it.'

'On top of it?' repeated Tiger.

'We need to dig,' said Ant. 'Max must have buried his watch for a reason.'

It was tough work using just their hands but, after toiling for what felt like an eternity, they found the blue wristband of Max's watch and carefully hauled it from the ground.

'Is it still intact?' Cat asked, as Tiger brushed the sand off. The slightest damage could strand them all in the dimension.

'It looks OK …' Ant replied.

Between them, they balanced the huge watch on their shoulders and, with their knees sagging, retraced their steps back to the edge of the square and ditched the box as soon as possible. It was too hazardous to grow back to normal size, so they had to continue to share the burden of the watch's weight as they made their way through the city. Progress was painfully slow, but finally they managed to get to the city wall again.

Back at the buggy, they reverted to normal size and swiftly removed the camouflage that had hidden it from view.

Tiger strapped Max's watch on to his wrist, next to his own. 'I'll keep it safe for you, Max,' he muttered.

They took their seats and buckled up; then Tiger fired up the engine.

'Have you got any more readings for Vilana?' Ant asked Cat.

Cat checked her watch once more. 'There's a new signal showing north-north-west,' she confirmed. 'If Vilana left the dimension, then she's come back for some reason.'

Whatever the reason, the friends knew it couldn't be good.

They drove in silence, Cat only occasionally giving directions to Tiger. Although retrieving Max's watch had been a major step forward, they still didn't know what had befallen their friend.

Then they had a setback. A group of roach scavengers travelling on foot had spotted the buggy as it moved away. The creatures quickly turned around and ran back towards the city.

'They've gone to raise the alarm,' Ant said gloomily. 'Do you think they'll try and follow us?'

'Absolutely. Another reason to get a move on!' Tiger said, stamping on the accelerator.

The journey took them across country, traversing a dune area and then up a steep escarpment to a plateau.

'We can get a bit more speed up here,' Tiger said with satisfaction. The surface was smooth and the rubbish piles easy to dodge.

The buggy raced along, the three friends alert for any clues that might lead them to Max. Soon they became aware of something new on the horizon, a glittering pinpoint of light which shone out valiantly against the dull textures of the desert floor.

'It's some sort of building,' Tiger said.

'A lighthouse?' Ant guessed.

'Err, haven't you noticed … there's no sea round here. Only a sea of rubbish,' Tiger pointed out. 'Why would there be a lighthouse with no ocean?'

'It looks more like … mirrors,' Cat suggested. 'A building made of mirrors.'

The friends drove up close and parked the vehicle. Then they climbed down from the buggy and cautiously approached the strange-looking monument. The closer they got, the more they could appreciate the extraordinary size of the place. It was huge – several hundred metres high – and was the same shape as a lighthouse, but with an outer curtain wall protecting it.

Not far from the building they found a strange titanium post, protruding from the ground. The metal marker was waist height and had a symbol printed on the top. They examined it closely.

'That's odd,' Ant said. 'This symbol looks like a dimension rip.'

Cat ran her fingers over the embossed marking on the small post. 'What does it mean?' she asked.

The others shrugged. For the moment it would have to remain just another mystery. They continued the few steps to the building. As they got closer, their reflections became distorted and twisted as if they were standing in a fairground mirror maze.

'Look at me!' Tiger whispered with a smile. His head was blown up like a balloon in the reflection.

'It's not the time to mess around,' Cat scolded. 'Look – all the mirrors are broken. I don't like the feel of this. Let's take a closer look inside.'

They entered a central courtyard where sunlight was fragmented and redirected in a thousand different directions.

Surrounded by mirrors, their own body movements were caught in dozens of the broken fragments every time they changed position. The effect was unsettling, as if they were being stalked by an army of clones.

'I ... don't like this place,' Ant whispered.

The air was quiet, still and menacing.

'Let's go inside the tower,' Cat said. 'The rip reading is coming from inside.' She led the way up a ramp, heading for the main entrance.

As the three friends walked cautiously into the building, they felt the floor flexing beneath their feet. A creaking sound of stressed metal and glass accompanied every step, so that they feared the whole edifice would crash down at any moment in a pile of lethal shards. They continued along a winding corridor for some distance, picking their way with care and spreading out so their weight wasn't focused in any one spot.

'The whole building feels like it's swaying,' Cat observed.

'But there's no wind outside,' said Ant.

They climbed up a sloping ramp.

'We're getting really close to the rip now,' Cat said, glancing at her watch.

Suddenly they heard a ghostly voice. Vilana. Her words echoed strangely through the building. 'I have chosen to imprison you in this dimension … but in the past, in a time when all was green and vibrant in this place. It will be nice for you to see how this planet used to be, don't you think?'

Then came another voice, screaming, 'No!'

'Max!' Cat whispered, horrified.

They picked up speed, moving faster in the direction of the voices.

'Goodbye, Max … forever!'

Cat, Ant and Tiger rounded a corner just in time to see Vilana strike the air with the Staff of Worlds, creating a new rip. She jumped through and the rip snapped shut behind her.

Ant froze to the spot. All the blood drained out of his face as he concentrated on the mirror wall behind where the rip had just vanished.

'I can see Max,' he whispered.

'Where?' asked Tiger, looking round, expecting to see him in the room.

'There!' Ant stepped closer to the mirror wall.

Cat and Tiger followed him and stared at the place on the wall he was pointing to. Cat took a sharp intake of breath.

Max was visible *inside* the mirrored structure, the transparent walls behind him revealing a verdant landscape of rolling hills.

'Max? Can you hear us?' shouted Cat.

Max stepped closer to the mirror wall that separated them. There was a frown on his face, as if he was concentrating hard. He was staring in their direction, but it wasn't clear whether or not he could see his friends.

'Max!' Tiger yelled his name at top volume.

Max's face creased slowly in recognition. He looked like he was able to hear *something*, but it was obviously faint to him and barely audible.

He placed his hand against the mirror wall and Cat matched it by putting her own hand on the same spot.

'He's been locked in another dimension by Vilana,' Ant said, as if coming to terms with it. 'Now she's gone …'

'So how come we can see him?' Tiger asked.

'The walls between dimensions could have been damaged by Vilana,' Ant suggested.

'So now the question is – how are we going to get him back again?' Cat asked. 'Any ideas?'

Chapter 7 – Sundir

'How about we just smash down the mirrors?' Tiger proposed. 'Wouldn't that open up a kind of home-made rip between the two dimensions?'

'I'm not sure it's such a great idea,' Ant replied. 'A hole like that definitely couldn't be fixed; it would be there forever. I think we've already done enough damage.'

On the other side of the mirror, Max sat down. They sat down, too, cross-legged in front of him.

'I doubt it will be so easy to smash that barrier between worlds anyway,' Cat added.

'But if we don't get him out of there, Max will be lost forever!' Tiger groaned, looking down at his wrist where he had strapped Max's watch next to his own. His brow furrowed as he stared at the watches. 'How about we ask the Weaver?' he said. 'Ant, can you get the communicator on Max's watch working?'

Ant nodded. 'No problem.'

Tiger unbuckled Max's watch and handed it to Ant,

who quickly got to work. Time ticked by as he tried to set up the connection with Aracnan, their friend and guide who was stuck in Tiger's bedroom, waiting for them to regain the Staff of Worlds.

Finally Ant had the link up and running. A holographic image of the Weaver appeared, emanating from the centre of Max's watch. Cat quickly described their situation to Aracnan.

'I know the building you are in,' he told them. 'It is a rip beacon, once an entry point for rip-travellers – immortals like me would meet there occasionally. It was a popular destination.'

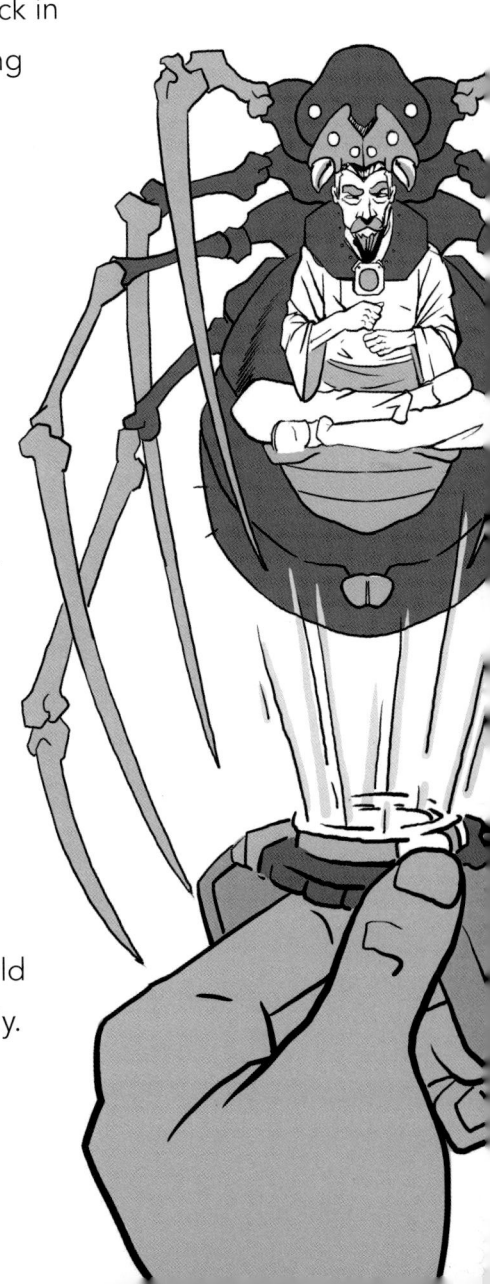

DIMENSION 0067
THE RIP BEACON

There were once rip beacons like this spread across the multiverse. Now only a handful remain, and the rip-travellers who used them have all but vanished. Beacons act like lighthouses, but instead of warning travellers away from dangerous rocks and shallow waters, they attract rip-travellers to them, lighting their way across the void between dimensions. Beacons are lit by a substance called sundir.

In their heyday, the beacons were a hive of activity. The tall glass towers attracted rip-travellers from near and far. Travellers would meet and swap stories about the dimensions they'd been to and the people they'd met, before travelling onwards to new adventures.

The rip beacon of Dimension **0067** was one of the most popular. It was taller than most, making it easier to locate.

SUNDIR:
Sundir is an unusual substance. Now difficult to come across, not much is known about it. It is rumoured it was once regularly used by rip-travellers to break down the walls between space and time.

'Max is trapped inside the building but in a *different* time,' Ant explained. 'We have his watch. What can we do to free him?'

'There is one possibility,' Aracnan said, after pondering for a moment. 'Many rip-travellers once used an element called sundir to help them cross dimensions. It's a useful substance, good for breaking down the walls of space and time.'

'Sounds dangerous,' said Ant.

'In the wrong hands,' replied the Weaver. 'Like most things. There was always a vial kept in store at that building, just in case of emergencies. There's a chance that some of it could still be kept there …'

'How do we use it?' Ant asked.

'You just pour it down the section of dimension wall you want to break into. But I warn you, it's feeble compared to the rip-jumping you're used to, and it only lasts for a few seconds. It sounds like you are under time pressure, my friends, so you'd better get searching right away!'

The three friends yelled to Max that they would be back soon, hoping that he could hear them.

'We'll have to split up,' Cat told the others. 'Try and find this sundir as quickly as we can.'

Ant and Tiger didn't need telling twice. Within

seconds, all three of them were sprinting through the empty rooms of the shattered mirror palace, desperately seeking the precious element. Tiger took the uppermost floor, darting from one room to another but failing to find any cupboards or nooks in which a vial could be concealed.

In the floors below, Cat and Ant were having the same problem; the mirror rooms were devoid of any real storage places, the walls just broken glass and little more. They tried tapping against the floors in the hope of finding a hidden cavity or false compartment, but there was no hiding place to be found.

'I've drawn a blank!' Cat told the others when they got back together. The others agreed.

Then Ant remembered something. 'The rip symbol was etched on that metal post outside!' he exclaimed. 'That could be a clue that the sundir is hidden there.'

The three friends hurried from the tower of broken mirrors, out through the courtyard and across to the mysterious titanium post.

'It must be locked inside somewhere,' Ant said.

Tiger stalked round the post, studying every centimetre of its surface. 'There's no way in! The entire post is just one smooth piece of metal, with the exception of the rip engraving.'

Cat looked thoughtful. 'It's got to be something to do with that icon surely. I don't believe it's just a marker …'

'That's it, Cat!' Ant cried. 'It's not just telling you what's here – it's also telling you how to get to it!'

Cat and Tiger looked up, not quite following.

'We need to open a rip. We've got Max's watch, so there's no reason we can't at least try.'

His friends nodded their agreement and carefully set their watches.

Within seconds, the familiar blue light appeared and the post in front of them disintegrated before their eyes. In its place emerged a stone podium and, on its top, an opaque glass container with a corked top.

Cat picked it up and shook it gently. 'Sundir,' she breathed as she gazed at the sparkling fluid inside. 'We did it! Great idea, Ant!'

'No time for congratulations now, Cat,' Ant reminded her, secretly pleased. 'We need to get back inside.'

The three friends were just about to head back into the building when Tiger suddenly saw a red warning light on his watch. He stared into the distance and noticed a line of dust hanging just above the horizon.

'There's movement out there!' he called. The others looked in the same direction.

'There's a dust cloud …' Cat used the magni-scope on her watch. 'Roaches!'

They stared towards the moving line, trying to gauge just how many vehicles were cloaked within the dust cloud.

'How long do you reckon we've got?' Tiger asked.

'About five minutes,' Cat guessed.

The friends raced back into the mirrored building, their hearts pounding. They had been fortunate to survive an encounter with the roaches in the buggy chase, but now it looked like half of Roach City was heading towards them. And it clearly wasn't a welcoming party they had in mind.

One floor. Two. Running up the stairways of mirrors, the three friends tried not to brush against the razor-sharp walls. The climb started to take its toll, and they were all breathing heavily by the time they got back to the room where they'd last seen Max.

'Where is he?' Cat stared around wildly, fearing they had lost the location of the adjoining dimension. Then she saw the familiar spot where Max was visible. 'This is the place!'

They started banging urgently on the glass and the thudding brought Max back to the dimension wall. He stood there looking out with an expression of determination.

'Step back, Max,' Cat yelled. 'We're going to try and create a hole in the dimension wall.'

The tension was rising. Tiger turned round to glance out of the window of the building; the roach raiders were getting closer and closer. The ground was beginning to judder with the weight of hundreds of buggies as they thundered across the plateau. Soon the whole building picked up the vibrations, the superstructure swaying to and fro as if at the point of collapse.

'This place is falling to pieces!' Cat cried. She

approached the dimension wall, getting as close as she could. 'You need to push against the wall as soon as I pour this fluid!'

Max nodded uncertainly.

Cat took the vial of sundir and uncapped it. A bright green curl of sweet gas crept into the air around them. She peered inside the vial; there was a small quantity of translucent liquid sloshing in the bottom.

Crack! Cat jumped and almost spilled the precious fluid. Just to her left, a mirror had flexed a bit too far, and shattered into hundreds of pieces. A hole appeared in the side of the building. Another wall disintegrated just an arm's length away. Ant was forced to jump upwards as yet another mirror tile began to crack beneath his feet.

'Do it now!' Ant called.

Cat raised the container and tipped the contents directly down the dimension wall. The fluid ran with a loud hiss down the shattered mirrored surface, causing a ripple effect that seemed to vibrate through the air.

Max jumped back in alarm, holding his hand to his mouth to protect himself from the sudden flurry of thick smoke.

'There's a split!' Tiger yelled in triumph. The dimension wall had opened up with a crack that was about a hand's width across. It didn't look very stable, but it was the best chance they had.

Max got the idea fast. He thrust his hand through the crack and tried to push through. But the wall was still stiff and unyielding on both sides of the fissure and he struggled to force it open.

'Pull his hand!' Cat yelled.

The three friends bunched up together and pulled with all their force. They dragged Max's wrist through. Sparks were flying around the impromptu rip-hole. Smoke was drifting up in a sinister fashion from his shirtsleeve.

A violent clamour from outside told the friends the roach raiders were getting closer.

'I've got his elbow!' Ant shouted.

'Push your shoulder through, Max!' Cat shrieked.

Screeching wheels came to a halt outside the building. Aggressive cries rang out as the roaches leapt out of their buggies.

Max's shoulder and head pushed through the small gap. Cat, Ant and Tiger were still pulling with all their might.

A roach spear came shooting through the window.

It embedded in the floor with a meaty *thwack*, just missing Tiger's foot.

Rocks began to rain against the exterior of the building, and soon the friends were overwhelmed by the crashing sound of breaking mirrors.

Worse still, Max was tiring. Pushing against the dimension wall was taking a heavy toll on his body; he was becoming pale and breathless.

'It's … no … good,' said Max.

'Don't give up, Max!' Ant cried. 'Keep pushing.'

But Max slipped back from the rip, away from them. Ant and the others looked on in horror. The crack was resealing before their eyes! Their only chance to get Max back was vanishing fast.

Then they heard the patter of fast-moving footsteps, the keratin clatter of antennae and carapaces bashing against the mirrored walls. The roaches were invading.

Cat looked inside the vial. There were just a few drops of sundir left.

'Here goes!' she cried. And with that she flung the last of the precious sundir on to the crack. The smoke rose again as a new fault quickly grew. Was it enough?

'Max!'

Chapter 8 – Rescue party

The first of the roach raiders entered the narrow corridor with blood-curdling shrieks. But the combined weight of the attackers caused a section of floor to give way and they vanished in a dramatic blizzard of broken mirror pieces.

'Now, Max! Now! Get to your feet!'

Max staggered upright and sluggishly pushed forward once again. Encouraged by the cries of the other three, he got both of his fists through the gap. Immediately he felt his wrists grabbed hard, and his arms were tugged towards the other dimension. Max began to push forcefully with all his might, ramming his head against the opening until his face emerged into the other dimension.

'One last heave!' Ant urged the others.

The others reached right inside the rip, grabbed Max underneath the arms and pulled.

Seconds later he was out and free, a great cry of delight echoing from all four friends as they were united once again. But there was no time for lengthy celebrations; another party of roach invaders had arrived and were pelting the friends with spears as they picked their way across the broken section of floor.

'Which way out?' Ant asked.

The maze of passageways in the mirrored palace was ever-changing, the walls and floors collapsing at every turn. They had no choice but to follow their gut instincts, running through the corridors and storming up the stairways with the roach raiders in close pursuit.

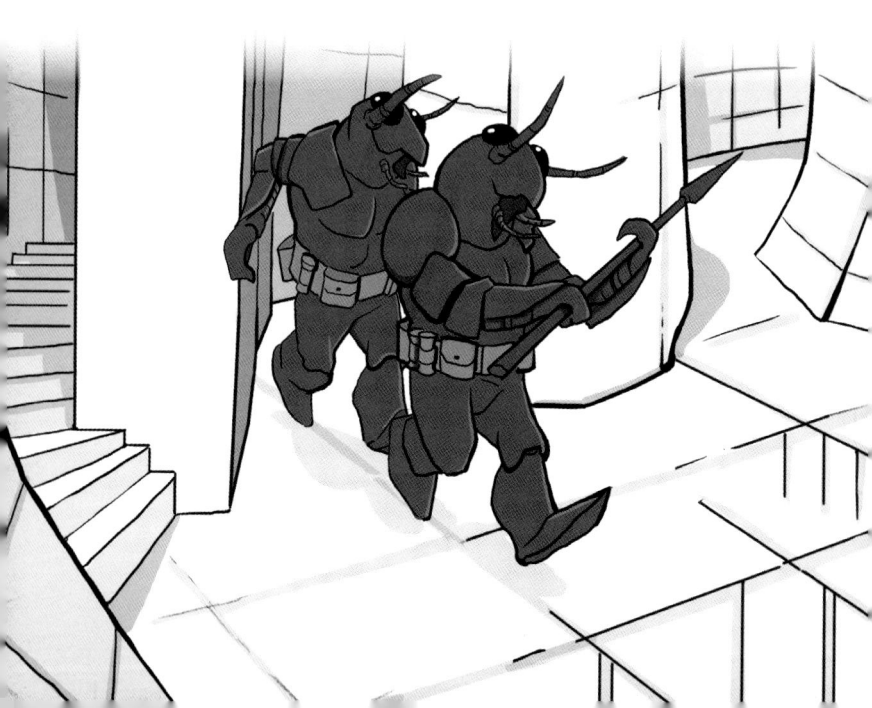

They scaled the stairs to the top of the building, the roaches following on as the whole structure swayed and shook ever more violently. Finally they reached the very top of the tower.

'There's nowhere to go!' Max cried, panting. 'We're trapped.'

For a moment it looked as if they were out of options. The room had no windows, and the only door was the one they had entered through. The clatter of the roach raiders as they climbed the stairway was getting louder. They were closing in fast.

'There's a tiny gap over there!' Cat pointed out. She had seen a place in the wall where a mirror had broken, creating a path through to the outside.

Tiger quickly handed Max his watch back, and the four friends shrank as fast as they could.

Seconds later they were micro-size and were running through the gap in the mirror wall. The roach invaders arrived just a fraction too late to stop them, smashing at the mirrors in their fury and trying to beat a way directly through the wall of the tower.

As shards of mirror flew through the air, Max and the others made their way along a small ledge that ran around the base of the turret. They inched their way along with great care, too terrified to look down at the vertigo-inducing drop beneath them to the glass-strewn surface of the desert floor.

At that moment a wonderful sound rang through the air: the throb of engines coming in close. The micro-friends looked out and saw a most extraordinary flying machine coming right up to the tower. It was comprised of four makeshift hot-air balloons, attached to the corners of an ancient aeroplane, which had clearly been discarded as junk long ago but was now brought back to life. The balloon canopies were made from colourful scraps of fabric and reclaimed materials.

Flying it was Seny. There was another flying machine just behind hers.

The friends acted fast, growing back to normal size just as the flying contraption lumbered past the turret.

'Climb on to this!' Seny called as she saw them. Moments later a rope ladder came snaking down and the four friends made their escape from the tower just as the roach invaders broke through the mirror wall in a flurry of spears. The flying contraption picked up speed and whisked the friends just out of range, the roach spears falling harmlessly into the sand.

'Climb up! I'll pull you in,' Seny called.

Max and the others made it into the safety of the cockpit.

'Welcome to wastelander airlines!' Seny told them with a big smile. 'We thought you might need a bit of assistance.'

'Hope you've got some decent in-flight movies?' Tiger said with a cheeky smile.

On the desert floor below, the roaches were climbing into their buggies and starting to follow the wastelander aircraft. They were livid at being cheated out of their prize.

'What about the roaches?' Cat asked. 'We can't go fast enough to shake them off, can we?'

'Oh, we can sort them out,' Seny said casually. She pulled back a compartment and revealed rows of hessian sacks. She opened one up to show the micro-friends thousands upon thousands of vicious-looking tacks.

'Take a sack and throw them far and wide,' she urged them. 'They won't get far on punctured tyres!'

Following this instruction with great pleasure, the friends shook the sacks so the tacks fell directly into the path of the pursuing buggies. The wastelanders in the other flying machine released their cargo of tacks, too. Soon thousands of sharp metal spikes were raining down.

One by one, the roaches found their tyres punctured, grinding to a halt in the desert sand as the wastelander flying machine flew majestically on.

Chapter 9 – New possibilities

By the time the machines made it to the wastelander settlement, the day was drawing to a close. Hundreds of Seny's fellow wastelanders came out as they heard the flying contraptions approach. As soon as they had landed they worked swiftly to dismantle the crafts and hide them in their underground storerooms.

The four friends knew the time had almost come to say goodbye to Seny, and they felt sad at the prospect of leaving her and her people in such a polluted wasteland. Then Cat had an idea.

'There is *something* we could give you to help your people,' Cat suggested, pulling out the vial from her pocket. 'There's one drop of sundir left in this container. If you could analyse its structure, you might be able to recreate it and make more.'

'Sundir?' Seny said with wonder. 'You mean it really exists? We've been trying to find out about it for ages. It's used for rip-jumping to other dimensions, right?'

'Correct,' Max told her. 'If you can manufacture

more you might even be able to go back in time …'

'And make some adjustments … try to stop the waste dumping before it even started!' Seny exclaimed with delight. 'It's worth a try, isn't it?'

Word quickly spread about the sundir and the wastelander scientific team came up from their lab to retrieve it. They carried the vial away with a tremendous sense of excitement and optimism.

Everyone in the settlement now had a new hope. It would be a challenge of their ingenuity to replicate the precious fluid. But that type of challenge was lifeblood to the wastelanders.

The friends walked a short distance away from the lake. It was time to report back. Max twisted the dial on his watch and moments later, to the shared relief of all the friends, Aracnan's hologram appeared.

'I see you have survived another dimension,' the Weaver told them. 'Have you managed to seize the Staff of Worlds from Vilana?'

'Not this time,' Max told him. 'But we will.'

'Then another dimension is waiting for you,' the Weaver told them. 'The sooner you get there the better. We don't want Vilana to have the least advantage in her quest.'

The four friends walked back to the lake and

exchanged warm goodbyes with Seny and her people. There was a great battle still to be won in this dimension if nature was not to be swamped by the ever-increasing mountains of waste. But, the micro-friends agreed, if it was down to ingenuity and courage, Seny and her fellow wastelanders would win through.

'Everyone ready?' Max asked.

What was waiting for them at their next destination, they didn't know. That was the danger. But it was also the thrill.

Four smiles cut through the night air. The blue light glowed as the rip appeared …

NEXT … The Last Dying Seconds